DIARY OF A WIMPY KID

by
Jeff Kinney

Teacher Guide

Written by
Linda Herman

Note

The 2007 Amulet Books hardback edition of the novel, © 2007 by Wimpy Kid, Inc., was used to prepare this guide. Page references may differ in other editions. Novel ISBN: 978-0-8109-9313-6

Please note: Parts of this novel deal with sensitive, mature issues. Please assess the appropriateness of this book for the age level and maturity of your students prior to reading and discussing it with them.

ISBN 978-1-56137-988-0

To order, contact your local school supply store, or—
Novel Units, Inc.
P.O. Box 97
Bulverde, TX 78163-0097

Web site: novelunits.com

Table of Contents

Skills and Strategies

Comprehension
Creative thinking, identifying attributes, predicting, inferring, supporting judgments, problem solving

Literary Elements
Story mapping, setting, characterization, conflict, theme, figurative language

Vocabulary
Syllables, sorting, definitions, synonyms, word maps, slang

Listening/Speaking
Discussion, oral presentation, drama

Writing
Creative writing, personal narrative, character journal, thank-you notes, journalism, short story, essay, poetry

Critical Thinking
Brainstorming, research, analysis, evaluation, compare/contrast, cause/effect

Across the Curriculum
Social Studies—relationships, middle-school culture, campaign advertising; Health—wrestling, weightlifting, mental health (bullying, self-esteem, jealousy, journaling); Music—music history; Math—computation; Art—design, illustration, basic shapes, comics, cartoonists

Genre: humorous fiction; "a novel in cartoons," or hybrid novel (between prose and graphic novel); diary

Setting: contemporary; Greg's home, neighborhood, and school

Point of View: first person

Themes: friendship, family relationships, middle-school life, popularity, gender differences, bullying, loyalty, coming of age

Conflict: person vs. self, person vs. person, person vs. society

Style: episodic narrative

Tone: humorous, ironic, conversational

Date of First Publication: 2007

Summary

Greg Heffley records the daily drama of his family life and first year in middle school in an illustrated journal—not to be confused with a diary. Greg is a regular kid with a deadpan sense of humor and a talent for drawing. He loves video games, hates responsibility, and wants to fit in at school, but his backfiring schemes keep him in trouble. As the middle child, Greg resents that his parents allow older brother Rodrick to pick on Greg, yet prevent Greg from picking on Manny, Greg's youngest brother and his parents' favorite. At school, Greg struggles with bullies, the mystery of girls, and the dead weight of a nerdy best friend named Rowley, all while scheming to increase his own popularity. Greg also frets about the "Cheese Touch," a condition similar to Cooties that involves a rancid piece of cheese. Oblivious to his faults, Greg's actions strain his friendship with Rowley—and just as Rowley's popularity is rising. However, when teenage bullies force Rowley to eat the Cheese, Greg protects his friend. In a show of loyalty, Greg willingly accepts the Cheese Touch and the dreaded consequences.

About the Author

Jeff Kinney was born in Maryland in 1971 and grew up in the Washington, D.C. area. He says he was a regular kid who had wimpy moments and that Greg Heffley is his "worst parts, amplified." Kinney always dreamed of becoming a cartoonist. He graduated in 1993 from the University of Maryland, where he switched majors from computer science to criminal justice to have more time to work on cartoons. His comic strip, *Igdoof,* was published in the campus paper, and he'd hoped the comic strip would be professionally syndicated. After many rejections, Kinney became an online game designer for the Family Education Network. "Wimpy Kid" was first introduced on their Funbrain.com Web site. Kinney can hardly believe the success of his "Wimpy Kid" series, the first of which will become a motion picture in 2010. In 2009, Kinney was honored as one of *Time* magazine's 100 Most Influential People in the World. He still works full time as an online game developer and virtual world designer and is the creator of Poptropica.com, a children's game site. Kinney currently lives in Massachusetts with his wife and their two sons.

Diary of a Wimpy Kid, along with other titles in the series, is a #1 *New York Times* Best Seller. The novel has won numerous awards including Book Sense Book of the Year, the 2007 Borders Original Voices Award, Nickelodeon Kids' Choice Award: Favorite Book, and is an ALA Notable Book. The novel is published in 28 languages with the German title translating as *Greg's Journal: I'm Surrounded by Idiots.*

Characters

Greg Heffley: lightweight, middle-school student; likes video games; writer and owner of illustrated journal

Rodrick Heffley: Greg's older brother; teases Greg; His heavy metal band is called Löded Diper.

Manny Heffley: Greg's younger brother; overprotected by his parents; His nickname for Greg is "Bubby."

Mr. Heffley: Greg's father; sports-oriented; hates heavy metal music and video games

Mrs. Heffley: Greg's mother; caring; strict; likes all music

Rowley Jefferson: Greg's best friend; loyal; naïve

Mr. Jefferson: Rowley's father; doesn't allow violent video games

Fregley: Greg's neighbor; the "weird kid"; uses a made-up language

Patty Farrell: know-it-all student; annoys Greg; plays Dorothy in the school production of *The Wizard of Oz*

Collin Lee: Greg's "backup friend" who befriends Rowley

Mr. Ira: Greg's geography teacher; edits Greg's comic strip

Mr. Winsky: school administrator in charge of Safety Patrols

Background Information

While working on Funbrain.com, Jeff Kinney never gave up on his dream of being a cartoonist. He thought that a book, in journal form, from the point of view of a kid in middle school would complement his simple drawing style. For the next eight years, Kinney kept a journal generating ideas from childhood memories and developing his ideas, jokes, and sketches into a publishable format. He intended the book to be an adults' nostalgic and ironic look back on the difficult middle-school years. He says, "I wanted to write a story about all the funny parts of growing up, and none of the serious parts." Then Funbrain.com needed a way to keep kids visiting their Web site during summer, and Kinney suggested "Wimpy Kid." Daily installments drew over 70,000 viewers per day. Despite the online success, Kinney still had doubts when Harry N. Abrams, Inc., offered to publish "Wimpy Kid" as a children's book series. He thought kids would not understand the irony of the book, though he now says, "But I've been alarmed and delighted that they do." He also points out that writing the book for an adult audience prevented him from writing down to kids and stressing moral lessons.

Diary of a Wimpy Kid is a hybrid novel, half comic and half novel. In hybrid novels, the illustrations advance the plot, and without them, the story wouldn't make sense. Kinney's illustrations include subtle meanings: girl characters look the same because Greg does not understand girls, while boy characters are drawn uniquely. A hybrid novel combined with the narrative style appeals to reluctant readers. Although he is sometimes criticized for the style, Kinney considers *Diary of a Wimpy Kid* as "a gateway to legitimate reading."

The following information regarding tone will enhance students' understanding of *Diary of a Wimpy Kid*. In the novel, Kinney uses the following types of humor:

- deadpan humor—a purposely flat delivery of humor with no amusement in the tone

- hyperbole—deliberate exaggeration

- irony—1) dramatic: when the reader knows something the character does not;
  2) situational: when the opposite of what is expected occurs; 3) verbal: what is said has a different meaning than it usually does, as in sarcasm or understatement; the character means the opposite of what s/he actually says

- sarcasm—a cutting remark designed to make fun of someone or something

- understatement—a statement for humorous effect that is restrained in ironic contrast to what might have been said; to really simplify something; the opposite of hyperbole

Initiating Activities

1. Comparisons: Read page 1 of the novel to the class. Ask students the following questions: What is the difference between a diary and a journal? Which would tell you more about the author's feelings? Which would tell you more about events? Have students apply this information as they read the novel.

2. Comprehension: In *Diary of a Wimpy Kid*, Greg is considered an "unreliable narrator." Though Greg writes truthfully, he records situations as he understands them. However, through his descriptions and illustrations, readers can infer what is really happening. As they read, students should list examples that show Greg as an unreliable narrator by completing the Inferences chart on page 24 of this guide.

3. Literary Devices: Explain to students that onomatopoeic words sound like what they mean (e.g., *buzz, clink, POW!*). Have students thumb through the novel looking at the illustrations for onomatopoeic words. Instruct students to create bookmarks that illustrate a school scene that would include sounds. Students should use written onomatopoeic words to convey the sounds.

4. Literary Analysis/Art: Discuss with students the role cartoons play in a hybrid novel, including how illustrations advance the plot and how every line in a drawing serves a purpose (see Background Information on page 5 of this guide). To prepare students to closely examine the illustrations as they read the novel, ask them to draw facial expressions depicting the following emotions: happiness, anger, fear, anxiety, surprise, pain, and mischievousness. You may wish to introduce cartoon terminology, such as speech and thought balloons, motion lines, and Symbolia (For example, sweat droplets indicate stress or exertion, "ZZZZ" indicates sleep, and light bulbs indicate ideas).

5. Predictions: Refer to the Prediction Chart on page 25 of this guide. Have students examine the cover of the novel and then predict what they think will happen in the story by giving the following words as clues: popularity, schemes, Cooties, bullies, family, and friendship. Students should continue to fill in their prediction charts as they read.

Vocabulary Activities

1. Syllable Sort: List the syllables of ten vocabulary words in random order on the board. Instruct students to combine the syllables into ten vocabulary words. You may wish to give clues, such as how many words contain two or three syllables.

2. Word Skits: Divide students into groups, and assign five vocabulary words to each group. Students should write skits that incorporate the meanings of the vocabulary words into their stories as well as use the words in dialogue.

3. Synonym Connotations: Assign vocabulary words to students that are adjectives or verbs. Students should find synonyms for the vocabulary words and then list them in order of connotations from mild to extreme (e.g., *walk, stroll, ramble, trudge, march, stomp*).

4. Word Maps: Have students complete a Word Map (see page 26 of this guide) for ten vocabulary words from the novel.

5. Story Slang: Discuss with students the definition of slang and how the meanings of words can change over time. Have students use a dictionary to compare the formal and slang definitions of the following words from the novel: *lame, crash, gross, bean, wicked, ratting*. Working in pairs, students should write two short stories, one using the formal definitions and the other using the slang.

September

Keeping a journal is Greg's mom's idea, and he is only making entries to avoid tedious questions when he becomes famous. Greg discusses his concerns about middle school, such as bullying, popularity, and avoiding the "Cheese Touch." He writes about his home life—his parents' expectations and their different styles of punishment, his older brother Rodrick, who plays in a heavy metal band and constantly tricks Greg, and his younger brother Manny, who never gets in trouble no matter what he does. Greg's best friend Rowley seems unconcerned about maintaining a decent image at school, but Greg runs for class Treasurer to increase his popularity.

Vocabulary
specifically
complicated
popularity
stress
racket
expectations
annoyed
gimmicks
pranks
appreciate
logic
dismantle
gadgets
violence
backfired
red-handed
sarcastic
offensive
inflate
political

Discussion Questions

1. Have you ever kept a journal or diary? Did you find writing down events helpful? Why does Greg act defensive about keeping a journal? (*Answers will vary but may refer to learning more about oneself. Greg clearly states that he is writing in a journal, not a diary, and that it is his mom's idea because he worries people will label him a sissy, especially if they discover he is recording his feelings in a diary.*)

2. Greg believes age differences in middle school contribute to bullying and thinks grade levels should "be based on height, not age" (p. 3). What is Greg's logic? How would you determine grade levels? (*Answers will vary. Greg believes big kids have an unfair physical advantage in middle school. Students should explain the pros and cons of their solutions, just as Greg realizes his solution based on height would result in short kids, like Chirag Gupta, remaining in first grade.*)

3. How is popularity measured in Greg's school? Why might Rowley not care about being popular? (*Popularity depends on a person's clothes, wealth, and looks. Answers will vary. Rowley may be unwilling to make changes to become popular, or he may be content focusing on things that matter most to him. He may not understand the importance other students place on popularity or not yet be mature enough to share those concerns.*)

4. Why do you think Greg explains the Cheese Touch? (*Answers will vary. This entry foreshadows events later in the novel. Discussion should cover how authors usually only include events relevant to a story, that the events Greg writes about are not random incidents and, that by the end of the novel, the events form a complete story. Also, the Cheese Touch is funny because it is so illogical and irrational.*)

5. Greg learns from Rodrick "to set people's expectations real low so you end up surprising them by practically doing nothing at all" (p. 15). What does this tell you about Greg? (*Answers will vary. Greg, like most kids his age, wants to do things the easiest way possible. He may like people's reactions when he "surprises" them. He also avoids having his parent nag him.*)

6. Why does Greg feel that Rowley hurts his image? Should Greg end his friendship with Rowley? (*Answers will vary. Greg thinks Rowley is dorkey and has immature habits and interests. Discussion should cover the consequences of ending a friendship, what the action would say about Greg's character, and circumstances that would make ending a friendship appropriate.*)

7. How does Greg feel about being the middle child? *(Answers will vary, but students should infer that Greg feels his parents treat him unfairly. Rodrick is allowed to play tricks on Greg, but Greg isn't allowed to play tricks on Manny.)*

8. What does the illustration at the top of page 31 tell you about Greg's dad? *(Answers will vary. Greg does not include Dad in his drawing, which reinforces his written entry that Dad does not like the heavy metal played by Rodrick's band. Greg believes that Mom, however, is more open-minded to music and would participate in a family band.)*

9. Which do you think is most fair, Dad's or Mom's style of punishment? Why? *(Answers will vary. Dad's style of not staying angry is easier for Greg to handle but does not seem to teach Greg any lessons. Mom's style of taking a few days to figure out an appropriate punishment forces Greg to think about his actions, though Greg spends more time worrying about the punishment than he does learning lessons.)*

10. What do you think is the purpose of the illustrations on pages 44 and 45? *(The illustrations advance the story's plot by giving examples of how Greg would like to change his situation at school. They let readers know more about Greg's character. He wants to impress the girls and have authority over or respect from the jocks.)*

11. Why were Greg's campaign posters considered inappropriate? Is buying votes by handing out lollipops fair? *(Answers will vary. Greg's posters are a personal attack on another candidate, rather than promoting Greg's abilities to be Treasurer. Bribery doesn't seem fair, though the candidate may be using the lollipops as a conversation starter to talk to other students about the election. Discussion could cover personal attacks and buying votes as common practices in elections and whether voters would respect candidates more if they behaved ethically.)*

12. **Prediction:** How popular will Greg be at the end of the school year?

Supplementary Activities

1. Literary Analysis: Begin a Character Attribute Web (see page 27 of this guide) for Greg. Add information as you read the story.

2. Health: Research self-esteem, and then complete one of the following activities: a) write an essay on what you think the relationship is between self-esteem and being popular at school, b) design a brochure to help younger kids increase their self-esteem, c) write a poem about what being popular means to you.

3. Personal Narrative: The trick Rodrick plays on Greg at the beginning of summer vacation is an event that actually happened to the author, Jeff Kinney. Write about a time you were pranked. Include a cartoon drawing with your narrative.

4. Civics: Choose a character from a novel, and imagine that character was running for student body president at your school. Create a campaign poster in support of the character's candidacy.

October

Greg is secretly glad when Mom rescues him and Rowley from the Chainsaw Alley guy at the Crossland High School haunted house. Greg decides to make money with a haunted house of his own, which results in a frightened neighborhood boy and Rowley being grounded. Greg's plans for scoring an enormous amount of Halloween candy are ruined because Mom insists he take Manny trick-or-treating and Dad pulls his trash-can-full-of-water trick. When high school students bully Greg and Rowley, the two friends hide in Gramma's house and taunt the teenagers.

Vocabulary

drenches
bailed
embarrassing
convert
advertisement
admission
budge
clogging
cranking
legitimate
refund
jealous
reflective
regretted
salvage

Discussion Questions

1. Greg writes, "I'm not sure Dad really understands the concept of Halloween" (p. 50). What is Dad's concept of Halloween? Why do you think Greg questions his dad's actions? (*Dad enjoys Halloween because he has fun playing tricks, though only on teenagers. Greg is not interested in the holiday's traditions or costumes, only the candy. He may also disagree with Dad now that he is becoming a teenager—and possibly subject to a drenching.*)

2. Mom embarrasses Greg when she bails him out at the haunted house. What does Greg mean when he says, "…but I'm willing to let it go this one time" (p. 53)? (*Answers will vary, but students should see the humor in Greg's false bravado. Greg is relieved that Mom rescues him from a frightening situation.*)

3. After being frightened at the Crossland High School haunted house, why does Greg scare Shane Snella at his haunted house? (*Greg only thinks of the money he and Rowley can make. Even when Shane Snella refuses to come out from under the bed, Greg doesn't make a connection between his fear in Chainsaw Alley and Shane's feelings.*)

4. Why doesn't Rowley understand Greg's play-by-play of Rowley's favorite TV show? (*The illustrations show Greg giving his opinions on what he sees, instead of telling Rowley what is actually happening.*)

5. Describe Greg's cowboy costume from the previous Halloween. What does this tell you about Greg? (*The costume consists of two baseball caps worn sideways in a poor attempt to resemble a cowboy hat. Answers will vary. Greg's priority is what is in it for him as shown by his elaborate plans to obtain candy, and little time is left for designing a costume.*)

6. How well do you think Greg handles the situation with the pickup truck full of high school kids? What would you have done in Greg's situation? (*Answers will vary. Greg yells out that he will call the police, which he immediately realizes is a mistake. He should have kept quiet and let the teenagers drive away.*)

7. **Prediction:** When and where will Greg and Rowley meet the high school kids again?

Supplementary Activities

1. Speaking: Greg is jealous of Rowley's Halloween costume. Research jealousy, and then lead a classroom discussion about your findings. Discuss ways to deal with a jealous friend.

2. Math: Greg's Halloween plan was to hit 152 houses in three hours. Because Manny, Dad, and the neighbors accompanied Greg, he only hit one house every 20 minutes. If Greg would have received 34 full-sized candy bars on his planned route, how many full-sized candy bars did he actually receive? Assume that houses giving out full-sized candy bars are evenly distributed throughout the community. (2 candy bars—Solution: 152 houses divided by 3 hours equals about 51 houses per hour; one house every 20 minutes equals 3 houses per hour; 51 divided by 3 equals 17 times as many houses; 34 candy bars divided by 17 equals 2 candy bars.)

November

Greg decides to bulk up to avoid being partnered with Fregley in the wrestling unit. When Mom and Dad won't buy Greg expensive exercise equipment until he proves his dedication, he makes his own equipment. Greg persuades Rowley to safety-test the equipment. Patty Farrell spoils Greg's plans to cheat on a geography test, and Mom insists he audition for the school production of *The Wizard of Oz*. Greg schemes to use his part in the play to take revenge on Patty.

Vocabulary
retired
volunteers
demonstrate
bulk
ashamed
enthusiastic
reps
dedication
phony
concentration
audition
soprano

Discussion Questions

1. Greg knows Gramma's house is rolled with toilet paper because of his actions and that it will take a long time to clean up. He writes, "But on the bright side, Gramma is retired, so she probably didn't have anything planned for today anyway" (p. 76). What is your reaction to Greg's comment? *(Answers will vary, but most students will either laugh at Greg's deadpan humor or think that Greg behaves insensitively.)*

2. According to Greg, a good training partner "push[es] you beyond your limits" (p. 91). What makes this scene humorous? How might Greg be good for Rowley? *(Answers will vary. Greg definitely pushes Rowley beyond his limits. When Greg finally rescues Rowley, Rowley leaves, presumably upset. The end result is Greg never has to work out. This scene illustrates the dynamic between Greg and Rowley. Greg plays tricks on Rowley, Rowley gets upset, and then Rowley forgives Greg. Since Rowley's parents seem even more protective than Greg's, Greg may seem adventurous and exciting to Rowley. Greg's shenanigans force Rowley out of his comfort zone and persuade Rowley to try new things.)*

3. What do the journal entries regarding wrestling tell you about Greg? *(Answers will vary. Greg is willing to put forth effort for his needs, such as studying wrestling to keep from being hurt or embarrassed in P.E. class; however, he likes easy solutions to problems. Greg puts more effort into planning than working. He looks for what he believes are quick fixes, such as high-tech exercise machines and weight-gain powder.)*

4. Is it Patty Farrell's fault that Greg flunks his geography quiz? What stereotype does Patty represent in alerting Mr. Ira to the map on the wall? *(Students should infer that Greg flunks the quiz because he did not study. Answers will vary. Patty becomes the "narc," the teacher's pet, or the class brain.)*

5. Should Mom make Greg try out for the school play? Should she consider Greg's feelings of not wanting to be embarrassed in front of the school? *(Answers will vary. Mom is doing what she believes is right to make Greg a well-rounded individual, and she knows he would never try some new things without encouragement. Mom is perpetuating a typical "mom" stereotype. Greg's unwillingness foreshadows his performance.)*

6. **Prediction:** How will Greg perform in *The Wizard of Oz*?

Supplementary Activities

1. Social Studies: Choose any style of wrestling (e.g., professional, Greco-Roman, freestyle, or women's). Write a brief history about the style, and explain its rules.

2. Health/Interviewing: Interview a doctor or personal trainer with experience in youth strength training. Ask about the benefits and risks of weightlifting for kids and teens. Then, write an article based on information gathered during your interviews and research. Include quotes from your interviews in your article.

3. Critical Thinking: Greg's mom always tells him to "be careful what [he] wish[es] for" (p. 100). Divide a sheet of paper into three columns. In the first column, list three to five things you wish for. In the second column, list possible positive outcomes of your wish. In the third column, list possible negative outcomes of your wish. Be sure to write humorously, as modeled in the novel.

December

Greg enjoys the school play, a disaster during which he deflects his embarrassing nickname of "Bubby" onto another student. Greg's Christmas is disappointing when others get everything they wanted and a mix-up prevents Greg from receiving "Twisted Wizard," the only thing he wanted. On New Year's Eve, Greg is banished to his room for teasing Manny, and he makes a resolution to never play with his younger brother again.

Vocabulary
degrading
humiliate
semiformal
performance
production
ad-libbing
deflect
bouquet
entertained
appropriate
charity
disappointment
hyping
resolution

Discussion Questions

1. Why does Greg predict the play won't go well? *(No one learns their lines because Mrs. Norton stands nearby reminding them what to say. She also creates confusion by adding new scenes and characters.)*

2. What are the consequences of Rodrick's and Manny's presences at the school play? *(When Manny yells "Bubby," Greg quickly deflects the embarrassment to Archie Kelly, who later is bullied about the nickname. Rodrick videotapes the performance. To avoid future humiliation from Rodrick, Greg refuses to sing. The other Trees stop singing, which contributes to ruining the play.)*

3. How do you know that the play does not entertain Greg's family? What is ironic about the situation? *(Mom throws away Greg's flowers. The accompanying illustration shows Mom with a "tornado" above her head, and everyone but Greg is frowning. The irony is that Greg didn't want to participate but ends up enjoying the play the most. Mom, who thinks Greg will improve to meet her expectations, ends up the most disappointed.)*

4. Based on Greg's parents' actions so far in the novel, do you think Manny receives every single thing he circled in the catalog for Christmas? *(Answers will vary. Mom and Dad have shown they raise their children in a proper manner—insisting on Greg being active and not immediately buying Greg a weight set until he proves his dedication. Most likely, Manny does not receive everything he asked for. Greg is exaggerating, looking at Manny through the eyes of a middle child who sees the youngest child as the "favorite." He also does not take into consideration that many toys for young kids cost less than those for older kids, resulting in more packages for Manny to open.)*

5. How would you rate Greg's Christmas? If you were him, would you feel sorry for yourself? *(Answers will vary. Greg's parents give him nice gifts despite the wrapping paper mix-up. By saving his special gifts for last, they attempt to give Greg a fun and merry Christmas. Though Greg is upset, he does realize that the Giving Tree guy is having an even worse Christmas.)*

6. What are the best kinds of gifts to give? Why? How would you judge the gifts that Greg gave to his family and Rowley? Have you ever received a "lame" gift? *(Answers will vary. Gifts that are personalized to the recipient show the sender cares enough to be thoughtful. A toy helicopter for Manny and a book about rock bands for Rodrick are thoughtful gifts from Greg. A "#1 Mom" cup and a "#1 Dad" hat are nice gifts though not as personal. Greg forgets to get a gift for Rowley but quickly re-gifts the* L'il Cutie *book that Rodrick gave him.)*

7. **Prediction:** What will Greg do with the Big Wheel?

Supplementary Activities

1. Drama: Working in groups, create a tableau, or frozen scene, from *The Wizard of Oz* performance in *Diary of a Wimpy Kid*. Design costumes and settings. Tell your group members how to pose, and then have them freeze in position. When you touch a group member, he or she should speak his or her character's thoughts until you touch them again. Perform in class, or tape your performance on video.

2. Social Studies/Critical Thinking: Find out if there is a program that helps needy people in your city. Brainstorm a list of useful items for the needy. Consider donating an item to your local program.

3. Creative Writing: Write a humorous poem about visiting relatives like Greg's Uncle Charlie. The relatives may be real or imaginary.

4. Comprehension: Imagine you are an advice columnist like "Dear Abby" and that the following letter will be printed in your newspaper column. Write a response to be published with the letter.

   Dear _____,

   I asked Uncle Charlie for a video game for Christmas, but instead he gave me a picture of himself. Mom is mad at me for not hiding my disappointment. Why do I have to pretend to be happy over a gift I don't want? Won't pretending to be happy encourage Uncle Charlie to get me another awful gift next year?

   Signed, Confused Kid

January

Greg creates a general form letter to simplify writing Christmas thank-you notes that results in awkward messages. He invents a game with the Big Wheel that ends with Rowley breaking his hand. Rowley's cast increases his popularity at school, especially with girls. Greg unsuccessfully attempts to use Rowley's newfound popularity to get the girls' attention for himself. A new, experimental class, Independent Study, is cancelled after Greg and the other boys spend time listing curse words, rather than designing a robot. Greg and Rowley sign up for the Safety Patrols in order to receive perks, such as bully protection, hot chocolate privileges, and time off from regular classes.

Vocabulary
gauze
infection
swarming
sympathy
bust
independent
impressed
valuable
contributors
perk

Discussion Questions

1. What do you think of Greg's fill-in-the-blank thank-you notes? *(Answers will vary. Students will probably agree that the notes get progressively more hilarious. Since letter-writing takes time, it is probably not an activity into which most boys Greg's age would put effort. His solution is quite clever, but as usual, Greg's efforts do not always produce his expected results.)*

2. Why doesn't Greg's "injury" earn him popularity like Rowley's broken hand? *(Answers will vary. A raging infection does not occur overnight; therefore, students probably do not believe Greg is injured and realize he is looking for attention. Infections are gross compared to broken bones and less likely to draw feelings of sympathy, as shown by Fregley's interest in Greg's injury.)*

3. How are Greg's journal entries regarding Independent Study an example of deadpan humor? Do you think Greg is trying to be humorous in his journal? *(Greg writes about the class period as if the boys are seriously working on their assignment; however, readers realize the boys are intentionally focusing on curse words. Greg even credits Ricky Fisher, the boy who knows the most bad words, as a valuable contributor to the project. Answers will vary. Greg writes as if he is telling the truth. Therefore, the humor comes from the reader's interpretation as much as the author's intent.)*

4. What can you infer about Greg from his comments on the movie, *It's Great to Be Me*? *(Answers will vary. Greg shares his own interpretation of the movie's message; he believes the message is that a person should not change anything about him or herself. Most likely, the movie's message is that people should be happy with who they are and not make changes to please others. The movie probably does not tell viewers to avoid changing bad habits and poor behavior. Greg thinks that some other students, especially bullies, need to change.)*

5. Becoming a Safety Patrol means Greg and Rowley will miss 20 minutes of Pre-Algebra. How do Greg and Rowley react differently to this realization? Which boy reacts as you would? *(Greg feels lucky to get a free pass from class in addition to the bully protection he expected. Rowley seems concerned about missing class. Answers will vary.)*

6. What funny thing happens during Rowley and Greg's first Safety Patrol experience? *(Answers will vary. One of the kindergartners being escorted home begins to smell bad. Greg suspects the kid has had an accident and leaves the situation for an adult to resolve.)*

7. **Prediction:** What trouble will Greg get into as a Safety Patrol?

Supplementary Activities

1. Comprehension: Friday's and Monday's journal entries tell about Rowley falling off the Big Wheel and wearing a cast to school. Pretend you are Rowley, and write about the Big Wheel incident from your point of view. Include illustrations.

2. Creative Thinking: Design a robot for Greg's Independent Study assignment. (Your robot does not need to work.) Create a model or drawing of what your robot looks like. List ideas of what your robot might do.

February

Greg and Rowley attempt to build the world's biggest snowman. But when Greg kicks Manny's snowman, Dad destroys Greg's huge snowball. Greg and Rowley initially work together for the cartoonist job in the school paper, but then they split up. Greg gets the position; however, the fame he expected does not happen after Mr. Ira edits his comic.

Vocabulary
slacked
piddly
pathetic
ambushed
ironic
celebrity
bogged
obvious
cretin
rad
decent
expanded

Discussion Questions

1. What record does Greg wish to hold in the *Guinness Book of World Records*? What record would you want to hold? Why do you think people like to hold records? *(Greg and Rowley want to build the world's biggest snowman. Answers will vary. According to Guinness World Records' editor, Craig Glenday, reasons include: childhood dreams, setting goals and challenging oneself to achieve them, human nature to push forward—e.g., exploration, medical research, to outdo others and expand one's limits, "Without knowing the extremities, it is impossible to know where you stand [in the world]" [from http://www.guinnessworldrecords.com/editor, active at time of publication].)*

2. Why does Dad destroy Greg's snowball? What results from Dad's actions? *(Dad is angry at Greg for destroying the new sod and because Greg destroys Manny's snowman. Dad uses actions similar to Greg's in an attempt to show Greg how Manny feels. Rowley gets angry that their huge snowball has been demolished. Greg is flabbergasted that Rowley gets mad at him for something Dad did.)*

3. What is irony? Why is the Whirley Street kids' ambush of Greg and Rowley considered ironic? *(Irony is a discrepancy between what is intended or expected and what actually happens. Greg and Rowley intend to ambush the Whirley Street kids; however, the Whirley Street kids ambush Greg and Rowley instead.)*

4. Greg writes that he wants to be the school paper cartoonist because he wants "to get in on some of that kind of fame" (p. 165). Can you think of another reason Greg might apply for the job? *(Answers will vary but should include that Greg likes drawing and is good at it based on the illustrations in his journal.)*

5. What differences do you see between Greg's and Rowley's comics? How do the three comic strips by other students compare to Greg's and Rowley's? *(Answers will vary. Greg is more interested in drawing than writing jokes; he invents the "Zoo-Wee Mama" idea to avoid writing punch lines. Greg's drawings are more sophisticated with well-drawn details, such as noses. Rowley*

enjoys writing humor, though his drawings are childlike compared to Greg's. When the two boys work separately, Greg's "Creighton the Cretin" comics are akin to satirical parody, making fun of a stupid character. Rowley's comics focus on humorous situations. The works of the other students resemble Rowley's comics as far as lack of drawing skills, and their comics are simplistic and juvenile compared to Greg's.)

6. Why does Mr. Ira heavily edit Greg's comic and to what effect? (Answers will vary. Greg's comic is satirically funny. The original version ridicules a stupid character and has adults exposing the character's weaknesses. Mr. Ira seems to like the caricature but not the parody and uses the comic strip as a marketing opportunity. He changes the text to promote the library's newly expanded Math and Science section, showing he does not really understand the purpose of a comic. Greg's hopes of gaining popularity ironically result in embarrassment.)

7. **Prediction:** Who will replace Greg as the school paper's cartoonist?

Supplementary Activities

1. Critical Thinking: Explain why Guinness World Records has entry restrictions such as the following:

   a) will recognize "first woman to walk to the North Pole," will not recognize "first British woman to walk to the North Pole"

   b) will recognize "longest car," will not recognize "most unique car"

   c) will recognize "oldest dog living," will not recognize "fattest hamster"

   [from http://www.guinnessworldrecords.com/member/is_it_a_record.aspx, active at time of publication]

2. Literary Analysis/Writing: Irony occurs when something happens that wasn't expected to happen. For example, Greg expects to ambush the Whirley Street kids but the Whirley Street kids ambush him instead. Write a short story or cartoon strip that uses irony.

3. Art: Create antismoking or other topic-related posters, and hold a classroom contest. Search the Internet for the use of humor in public service announcements, and refer to page 166 of the novel to see how humor and/or shock can be effective in a message. Your teacher may be the judge, or classmates can vote on the winning poster.

4. Literary Analysis: Mort Walker, a famous cartoonist, wrote a book titled *The Lexicon of Comicana*. In his book, Walker made up humorous names for the symbols found in comics and cartoons. Locate examples for each of the following symbols in *Diary of a Wimpy Kid*.

   • Plewds: sweat drops around a character's head

   • Briffits: clouds of dust that show action, such as running

   • Squeans: starbursts or circles indicating a character is dizzy or sick

   • Wafterons: wavy, rising lines signifying a smell

   • Agitrons: wiggly lines around a character that imply shaking

   • Blurgits and swalloops: curved lines before or after a character's limbs showing action

March–June

Rowley is suspended from Safety Patrols for terrorizing kindergartners, when it was actually Greg who chased the kids with worms. Greg does not want to tell the truth, but Mom tells him "to do the 'right thing,' because it's our choices that make us who we are" (p. 182). Greg decides the right thing to do is let Rowley take the blame. Rowley becomes popular as school cartoonist with "Zoo-Wee Mama" comics. Tension between Rowley and Greg increases when Rowley refuses to give Greg any credit for the comic idea. The high school students from Halloween night force Rowley to eat the Cheese; Greg's plea that he's allergic to dairy products spares him the same fate. When classmates realize the Cheese is missing, Greg protects Rowley's reputation by claiming to have thrown away the Cheese. Greg now has the Cheese Touch, though it isn't as bad as he'd feared. Rowley and Greg are friends again, and Greg vows to keep Rowley's ego in check by reminding him of the Cheese incident.

Vocabulary
witnessed
disrespected
privileges
pry
anonymous
culprit
promotion
maniac
immortal
execute
chaperone
foiled
hocus-pocus
taunting
theories

Discussion Questions

1. Mom tells Greg that he "should try to do the 'right thing,' because it's our choices that make us who we are" (p. 182). What does Greg decide is the right thing to do regarding the worm-chasing incident? Considering his mother's advice, how are Greg's actions humorous? *(Greg decides to let Rowley "take one for the team this time around" [p. 183]. Answers will vary. Greg's main concern seems to be as trivial as hot chocolate privileges. In middle school, all privileges seem to carry significant weight. This is part of the author's parody of middle school. The trivialization of his friendship with Rowley is understatement [a type of humor] because the reader knows that the friendship is actually important to Greg. Discuss whether students see life as Greg does: Everyone gets away with stuff except for you.)*

2. Why doesn't Greg tell Mr. Winsky the truth when he knows he will eventually be identified as the real culprit in the worm-chasing incident? *(Answers will vary. Greg usually takes the easiest way out, which in this case is to keep quiet. Though Greg knows he will be in trouble, he either hopes he will get lucky and the truth won't come out, or he is willing to delay the inevitable. Intuitive readers know that once again Greg's choices, as in many episodic sitcoms, drive the humor in the plot, often with disastrous results.)*

3. When Rowley is accused of terrorizing the kindergartners, his punishment is a one-week suspension from Safety Patrols, yet Greg's punishment results in permanent removal from Patrols. How do you think Mr. Winsky decides on each boy's punishment? *(Answers will vary. Mr. Winsky may consider a one-week suspension as the appropriate punishment for the incident but thinks Greg deserves a harsher punishment for not telling the truth. He seems to base punishments on character, as shown by Rowley's promotion for handling himself with dignity.)*

4. Greg thinks Rowley needs a lesson in loyalty and that Rowley is acting like a jerk. Do you agree with Greg? What can you infer from Rowley's actions? *(Answers will vary. Some students may agree with Greg, although most will realize Greg's actions are hypocritical, as he has not been a very good friend to Rowley, either. Rowley seems to have had enough of Greg. By becoming friends with Collin Lee, Rowley could be sending a message to Greg, or he may be ready to permanently end his friendship with Greg.)*

5. Does Greg have many friends? Support your answer with information from the novel. What is your experience with school friendships? *(Greg does not have many friends. Throughout the novel, Greg has only spent time with Rowley. Collin Lee, Greg's backup friend, befriends Rowley. Hilariously, Fregley is the only person Greg can think of when he wants to show Rowley that he, too, can get a new best friend. Answers will vary.)*

6. Why is Greg searching through Rodrick's things? How is Rodrick's yearbook important? *(Answers will vary. Greg is bored because, without Rowley, he does not have any friends to hang out with. Rodrick has labeled everyone in his yearbook as a jerk or as cool. The yearbook gives Greg the idea to be voted a Class Favorite to increase his popularity.)*

7. Rowley does not give Greg any credit for "Zoo-Wee Mama" comics even though the boys came up with the idea together. Do you think this is fair? *(Answers will vary. Some students may feel Rowley is justified since Greg let him be blamed for the worm-chasing incident and since Greg has treated him unduly in other ways. Others may think it wrong not to give proper credit and that Rowley's ending the friendship is sufficient revenge.)*

8. Is there a difference between sibling rivalry, such as Rodrick picking on Greg who, in turn, picks on Manny, and the high school students bullying Greg and Rowley? *(Answers will vary. Bullying is an act of aggression against a weaker person and is always wrong. According to this definition, making Rowley eat cheese is wrong. Sibling rivalry, however, is normal and can even teach kids how to resolve conflicts. Many siblings bully without intention, such as Greg's impulsive destruction of Manny's snowman.)*

9. At the beginning of the novel, the thought of having the Cheese Touch stresses Greg. Do you think he is telling the truth at the end of the novel when he writes that "having the Cheese Touch hasn't been all that bad" (p. 216)? *(Answers will vary. Greg often covers up his real feelings by finding bright spots in situations, and he says "Honestly" when readers can see he is not being honest. For example, Greg writes that he's better off without Rowley, though he is obviously bored enough to search Rodrick's room. While Greg may be pleased to avoid the square dance unit, having a lunch table to himself probably isn't fun. However, Greg may have learned that sometimes when our worst fears happen, it isn't as bad as we expected.)*

10. Do you think Rowley should have expressed his appreciation that Greg hid the truth about the missing Cheese? If you were Rowley, would the Cheese incident make you forgive Greg and want to be friends again? *(Answers will vary. Discussion could cover what Rowley's thoughts may be: Does he now owe Greg? Will Greg be a better friend in the future? Or should this simply count as payback for all the things Greg has done to Rowley?)*

11. What can you infer from the differences between the illustration on page 27 and the one on page 216? *(Answers will vary. Greg and Rowley's friendship is back to normal. The earlier illustration shows Greg's annoyance with Rowley and his lack of gaming skills. The second illustration shows Greg smiling, presumably happy to have his friend back.)*

12. Do you think Greg resents Rowley's rise in popularity? *(Answers will vary but should include that Greg is resentful, as shown by him throwing away the yearbook, which features Rowley as Class Clown.)*

13. To protect Rowley, Greg won't say what happens to the Cheese. Instead, he writes coded journal entries: "They made Rowley _ _ _ the Cheese" (p. 210) and "...I'll just remind him that he was the guy who ate the _ _ _ _ _ _" (p. 217). Do you see any comedy in Greg's plan to hide the truth? Can you think of a better way to protect Rowley? *(Anyone reading Greg's journal can look at the two coded sentences together and know that Rowley ate the Cheese. Answers will vary.)*

14. **Prediction:** Will Greg keep Rowley's secret about eating the Cheese?

Supplementary Activities

1. Writing: Everyone comes up with crazy theories about why the Cheese is missing. Write a school newspaper article reporting the event. Include interviews with Greg's classmates.

2. Literary Analysis: Complete the Literary Devices chart on page 28 of this guide.

3. Compare/Contrast: Originally, Greg's adventures were published online at http://www.funbrain.com/journal/Journal.html?ThisJournalDay=1&ThisPage=1 (active at time of publication). Compare one or two of your favorite parts from the novel with the online version. Write a brief explanation of the differences between the two versions, and tell which you like best.

4. Comprehension: Write the opening to a story about what would happen if Greg had also been forced to eat the Cheese. Write for five minutes, and then exchange papers with the student next to you. Read what that student wrote, and add to his or her story. After writing for another five minutes, exchange papers with a different student. Continue exchanging papers and adding to what others have written. Return stories to the original writer. Write a conclusion to the story that you started. Read the finished story to the class.

5. Writing: The author of *Diary of a Wimpy Kid* wishes he'd kept a journal as a kid. Start your own journal. Use it to learn about yourself as you grow up and to enjoy when you are an adult.

Post-reading Discussion Questions

1. The author of *Diary of a Wimpy Kid* states that Greg is not a role model. How would you describe Greg? *(Answers will vary. Greg is a regular kid with regular concerns about surviving middle school and family life. As depicted by his elaborate schemes, Greg is intelligent; however, he quickly loses interest in his often unrealistic goals. He usually chooses the easiest path or what's best for him. In interviews, Jeff Kinney said he wrote the novel for adults as a humorous, nostalgic look back on their middle school years. Only after the novel was complete did he realize that young readers can relate to Greg. He exaggerates Greg's life, but the reader still gets a sense that being a pre-teen is scary. Other kids are unreliable, adults are bothersome, and one's skills and talents are seldom recognized.)*

2. How does the desire for popularity create internal and external conflict for Greg? *(Answers will vary. Greg's internal conflicts include stress about the Cheese Touch and concern that Rowley is negatively affecting his image. He must decide whether to let Rowley take the blame for the worm-chasing incident and whether he should tell the truth about the Cheese incident. External conflicts arise when Greg's schemes to improve his status backfire. Examples include running for Treasurer, attempting to take advantage of Rowley's popularity increase, losing his Safety Patrols position, wanting to be voted Class Clown, and becoming the school paper's cartoonist.)*

3. By the end of the novel, has Greg learned to appreciate his friendship with Rowley? *(Answers will vary. Greg could have destroyed Rowley's newfound popularity by telling others that Rowley ate the Cheese. Instead, he chooses to protect his friend and damages his own popularity when he fakes having the Cheese Touch. Greg is loyal to Rowley in the end, and the illustration on page 216 depicts his joy that the friendship is back to normal. However, Greg does not learn the lessons he should have and even notes that Rowley never acknowledges Greg's good deed. Based on Greg's final journal entry, some readers may wonder if he will use the Cheese incident to manipulate Rowley.)*

4. Can you tell when the story takes place? Why do you think the author did not mention a specific time period? *(Answers will vary. The location of the story is never provided. The story is contemporary as shown by the inclusion of computers and video games; however, generic terms rather than dateable brand names are used: e.g., "game system" and "personal music player," instead of Game Boy and iPod. By not dating the book, the author ensures that readers of different age groups relate to the story, whether from nostalgic or contemporary viewpoints, and that the novel will remain relevant longer.)*

5. What are the novel's themes? How are these messages presented to readers? *(friendship, family relationships, middle-school life, popularity, gender differences, bullies, loyalty, growing up; Answers will vary. The story does not focus on or spell out moral lessons for readers. Instead, the author uses Greg's deadpan humor and irony to communicate the novel's themes. Readers understand Greg's life lessons, though Greg does not. Greg thinks he is clever, however, the reader sees the natural consequences of his actions and the reactions of others. For example, Greg never makes the connection between Rowley ending their friendship and letting Rowley be blamed for the worm-chasing incident. Greg still believes that Rowley betrayed him.)*

6. Review your Inferences chart (See Initiating Activity #2 on page 6 of this guide). Is using an "unreliable narrator" an effective way to tell a story? Did you enjoy working out differences between what Greg writes and what the illustrations show? *(Answers will vary. Though Greg writes in a truthful tone, readers are aware of what he misses and that he often exaggerates the importance of events, as shown when he dreads the Cheese Touch and then downplays it when he finally gets it. The illustrations advance the plot, providing additional details to Greg's writing. Greg's drawings allow readers to make inferences between what Greg reports and what actually happens. Drawings and school comic strips provide insight into Greg's personality, as do his choice of which events to record. An unreliable narrator can provide a humorous twist to storytelling.)*

7. Does Greg keep a diary or a journal? (See Initiating Activity #1 on page 6 of this guide). Did he enjoy writing in it? *(Answers will vary, but students should infer that Greg kept a diary. His writings and illustrations are of a personal nature. In addition to including his feelings, Greg writes about everyday incidents that only matter to him, as opposed to events with historical importance. Most likely, Greg enjoys keeping a diary with drawings since he made entries almost every day.)*

8. Do you think Greg will be famous one day? Why or why not? *(Answers will vary. Since Greg is creative and artistic, he could become famous as a cartoonist.)*

9. Some book reviewers criticize *Diary of a Wimpy Kid* because Greg does not learn any lessons and does not feel regret for his bad behavior. Do you agree or disagree with these critics? Does this affect your enjoyment of the novel? *(Answers will vary. The novel is a humorous look at the difficult middle-school years and is not intended to be taken seriously. Readers can relate to Greg, whether they too make wrong decisions or recognize similar behavior in others. Students will probably agree that the novel is an enjoyable, light read.)*

10. Describe Jeff Kinney's use of humor. Provide examples from the novel. Does his style of humor appeal to you? Consider both the text and the illustrations. *(Answers will vary. Some may describe the diary as filled with rude humor. Some students may point to the humor of the characters: Rodrick the jerk, Rowley the doofus, Mr. and Mrs. Heffley the dweebs, etc. However, some students may focus on the situations: haunted houses, wrestling, dangerous downhill games, toxic cheese, etc. Most students will say they enjoy the cartoons on almost every page. Reactions will vary from finding the humor amusing to laugh-out-loud funny.)*

11. *Diary of a Wimpy Kid* is the first book in a series and is being made into a movie. Will you read other books in the series? Will you see the movie? Why or why not? *(Answers will vary.)*

Post-reading Extension Activities

Writing

1. Compare Greg to a superhero in a comic. Write about what a meeting between the two characters would be like and what they might say to each other.

2. Create a poem about doing the right thing. Include why doing the right thing is often difficult.

3. Write an e-mail to Greg. Give your advice on what he should do to become popular at school.

4. Write a personal narrative about a time you made up with a best friend. Compare it to how Greg and Rowley mend their friendship.

Art

5. Invent an award to give to the novel (most funny, best cartoons, etc.), and design a medal for your award.

6. Learn drawing basics through the use of simple shapes, such as rectangles, triangles, and circles. With your teacher's permission, visit online tutorials that apply this technique. Choose an interesting object to draw.

7. Create a humorous comic strip suitable for a school newspaper. Use a computer drawing program, if available. Contribute your comic strip to a class comic book.

Speaking

8. Participate in a classroom discussion about idioms. Give examples from *Diary of a Wimpy Kid* as well as their meanings (e.g., "gets too big for his britches" [p. 217]). Brainstorm common idioms, and then create new ones.

9. Present a review of a video game. Tell whether you would recommend the game, and explain why.

Research

10. Create a health pamphlet about the changes faced by middle-school kids (i.e., physical, internal, external, and social). Use printed sources, the Internet, and interviews for your research. Include facts, opinions, and personal experiences (yours or others').

11. Read about the field of music history. Include visual displays and brief reports on various composers or styles. Explain the meaning of music to individuals or society as a whole.

12. Write a biography about a famous cartoonist. Draw a copy of the cartoonist's work to include with your report.

Assessment for *Diary of a Wimpy Kid*

Assessment is an ongoing process. The following 12 items can be completed during study of the novel. Once finished, the student and teacher will check the work. Points may be added to indicate the level of understanding.

Name _____ Date _____

Student	Teacher	
_____	_____	1. Complete the Cause and Effect graphic organizer on page 29 of this guide.
_____	_____	2. Compare and contrast Greg and Rowley by completing the Flock Together chart on page 30 of this guide. Then, write a paragraph about which boy you would rather have as a friend and why.
_____	_____	3. Write an essay on whether Greg shows any character growth by the end of the story. Include the reasons why he did or did not learn any lessons. Use information from the novel to support your answer.
_____	_____	4. Complete the Story Map on page 31 of this guide.
_____	_____	5. Create a collage illustrating Greg's experience as the middle child.
_____	_____	6. Write a poem or song about middle school. Share your poem or song in class.
_____	_____	7. Complete The Five Senses chart on page 32 of this guide. Use a scene such as the wrestling unit in Phys Ed or Greg's visit to the Crossland haunted house to complete your chart.
_____	_____	8. Describe how the illustrations in *Diary of a Wimpy Kid* help explain the novel.
_____	_____	9. Choose a theme from the novel, and explain to the class how it is developed.
_____	_____	10. Write three paragraphs on whether you think Greg is a wimpy kid. Support your answers with examples from the novel.
_____	_____	11. Complete the Rate This Novel chart on page 33 of this guide.
_____	_____	12. Review your Prediction Chart, Story Map, and other graphic organizers. Correct all quizzes, tests, and vocabulary activities.

Inferences

Directions: Complete the chart below with examples showing that Greg is an "unreliable narrator." Write a brief summary of Greg's description of a situation in Column 2 and the page number where it can be found in Column 1. In Column 3, explain what is really happening. (Example: On page 2, Greg states he is keeping a journal because it will come in handy when he is famous. The truth is that Greg enjoys writing in the journal, as shown by his numerous, daily entries.)

Page	What Greg thinks is true	What you think is really happening

Prediction Chart

Directions: Complete the chart below as you read the novel.

What characters have we met so far?	What is the conflict in the story?	What are your predictions?	Why did you make these predictions?

Word Map

Directions: Complete the word map below by filling in information for the chosen vocabulary word.

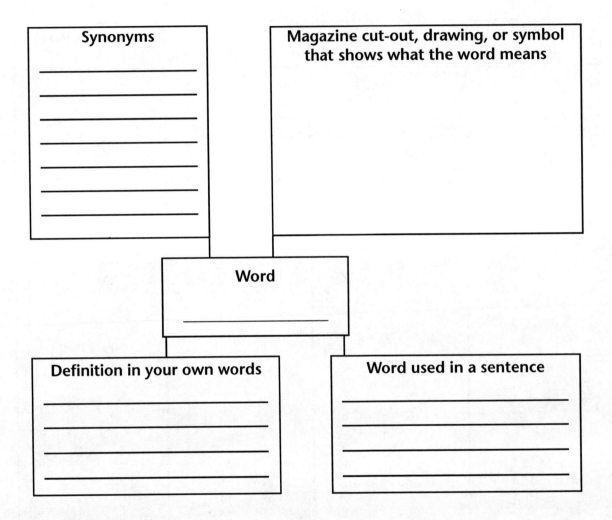

Character Attribute Web

Directions: The attribute web below will help you gather clues the author provides about a character in the novel. Fill in the blanks with words and phrases that tell how the character acts and looks, as well as what the character says and feels.

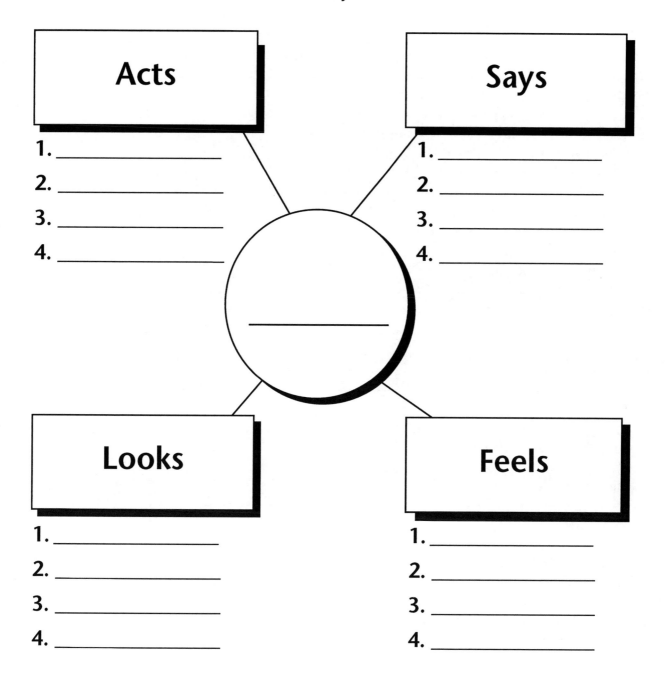

Literary Devices

Directions: Authors use literary devices to make their writing interesting and descriptive. Read the definitions of the literary devices listed below, and then find an example of each in the novel. Include the page number where you found the example.

Literary Device	Example
Flashback: The story switches to an event from the past, and then returns to the present. (Look for clues such as "She remembered the last time..." followed by a scene from the past.)	
Foreshadowing: An event is hinted about before it happens. (Example: His plan would work unless his mother found out about it.)	
Metaphor: A comparison is made between two unlike objects. (Example: He was a human tree.)	
Simile: A comparison is made between two unlike objects using the words *like* or *as*. (Example: The color of her eyes was like the cloudless sky.)	
Onomatopoeia: Words sound like what they mean. (Examples: buzz, hiss)	
Idiom: A phrase or expression that has a meaning different from the individual words that make up the phrase. (Example: It's raining cats and dogs.)	

Cause and Effect

Directions: Write four events from the story, and then list the effect of each event.

Cause	Effect

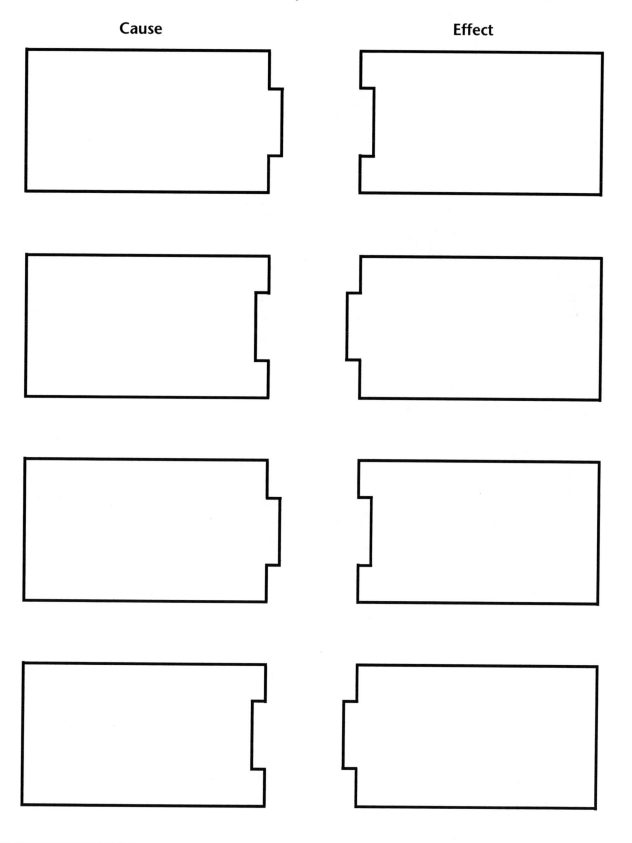

Flock Together

Directions: On each boy's feather, explain how he is similar to his friend. On the lines below the feathers, explain how the two boys are different from each other.

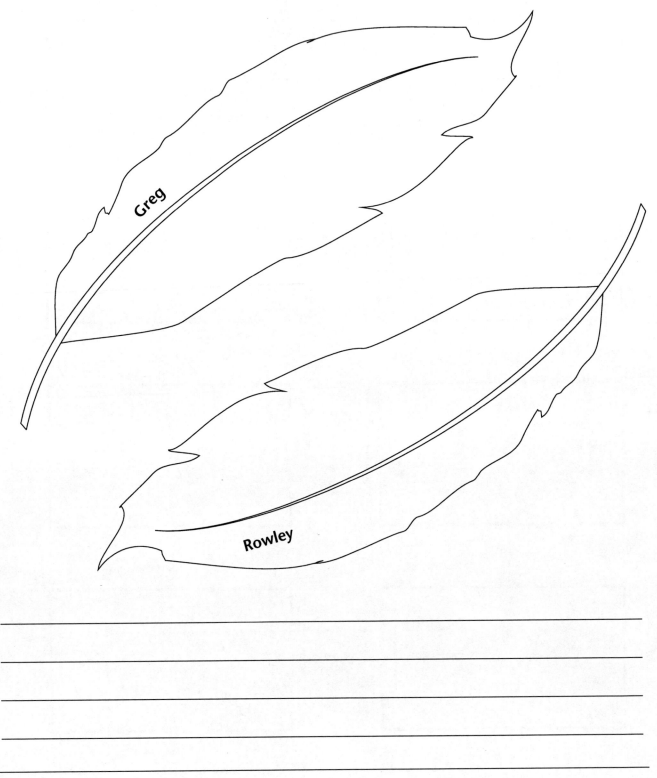

Story Map

Directions: Complete the story map below for *Diary of a Wimpy Kid.*

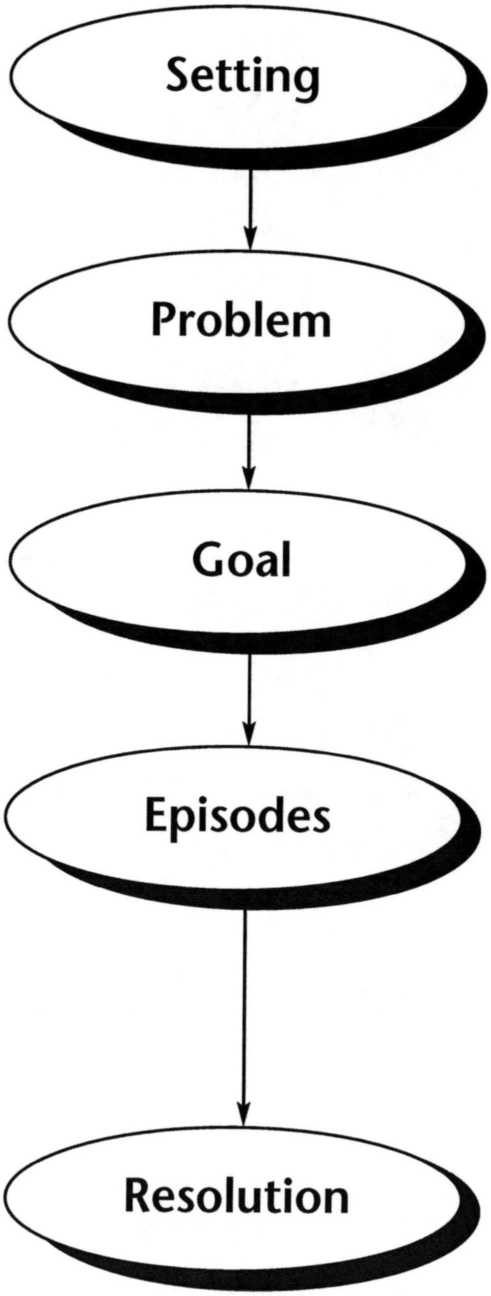

Characters_____

_____

Setting

Time and Place_____

_____

Problem

Problem_____

_____

_____

Goal

Goal_____

_____

_____

Beginning ⟶ Development ⟶ Outcome

Episodes

_____

_____

_____

_____

Resolution_____

Resolution

_____

_____

_____

The Five Senses

Directions: Choose a character from the novel, and circle one of the five senses shown. On the lines below, describe what the character experiences through the chosen sense. Use a scene such as the wrestling unit in Phys Ed or Greg's visit to the Crossland haunted house to complete your chart.

Character: _____

_____

_____

_____

_____

_____

_____

Rate This Novel

Directions: How would you rate this novel? How clear were its ideas and characters? Use the scale below to respond to each item. Discuss your answers with the class.

1 ——————— 2 ——————— 3 ——————— 4 ——————— 5 ——————— 6
very clear   very unclear

Rating

1. description of the setting _____

2. setting's importance _____

3. main character's goal _____

4. main character's problem (why he cannot reach the goal) _____

5. main character's plan to solve the problem _____

6. main character's thoughts _____

7. description of secondary characters _____

8. small details of the story _____

9. resolution of the problem at the end of the novel _____

10. novel's main message _____

Linking Novel Units® Lessons to National and State Reading Assessments

During the past several years, an increasing number of students have faced some form of state-mandated competency testing in reading. Many states now administer state-developed assessments to measure the skills and knowledge emphasized in their particular reading curriculum. The discussion questions and post-reading questions in this Novel Units® Teacher Guide make excellent open-ended comprehension questions and may be used throughout the daily lessons as practice activities. The rubric below provides important information for evaluating responses to open-ended comprehension questions. Teachers may also use scoring rubrics provided for their own state's competency test.

Please note: The Novel Units® Student Packet contains optional open-ended questions in a format similar to many national and state reading assessments.

Scoring Rubric for Open-Ended Items

3-Exemplary	Thorough, complete ideas/information Clear organization throughout Logical reasoning/conclusions Thorough understanding of reading task Accurate, complete response
2-Sufficient	Many relevant ideas/pieces of information Clear organization throughout most of response Minor problems in logical reasoning/conclusions General understanding of reading task Generally accurate and complete response
1-Partially Sufficient	Minimally relevant ideas/information Obvious gaps in organization Obvious problems in logical reasoning/conclusions Minimal understanding of reading task Inaccuracies/incomplete response
0-Insufficient	Irrelevant ideas/information No coherent organization Major problems in logical reasoning/conclusions Little or no understanding of reading task Generally inaccurate/incomplete response

Notes

Notes